WAXING AND CARE
OF CROSS-COUNTRY SKIS

M. Michael Brady

Wilderness Press
Berkeley

Photos by Frits Solvang except as noted
Drawings by Petter Bratvold except drawing on p. 8 by Bob Bugg
Cover photo by Frits Solvang
Design by Thomas Winnett
Cover design by Larry Van Dyke

Library of Congress Card Catalog Number 84-52654
International Standard Book Number 0-89997-048-6

Printed in the United States of America

Published by Wilderness Press
2440 Bancroft Way
Berkeley, CA 94704-1676
(415) 843-8080

Write for free catalog

Library of Congress Cataloging-in-Publication Data

Brady, M. Michael.
  Waxing and care of cross-country skis.

  1. Ski waxing. I. Title.
GV855.5.W36B72 1986   796.93'028   86-24561
ISBN 0-89997-048-6

CONTENTS

SORRY, NO WOOD

Nostalgia for wood skis aside, modern plastic-based fiber-glass skis are better in almost all respects, including ease of waxing. Wood ski bases absorb water from snow, which often complicates waxing as wax doesn't stick to wet surfaces. Preventing moisture absorption is a messy business, as it involves frequent tarring of bases. Though many rustics enjoy that aspect of cross-country skiing, for most skiers it's an art best forgotten.

WHY WAX?

"The gliding of skis and sled runners on dif-
ferent snows is an extremely difficult subject."
— Fridtjof Nansen,
Arctic explorer, 1930.

Modern skis and waxes eliminate the problems that concerned
explorer Nansen, yet much about waxing still seems shrouded in
mystery. Recent racing techniques, such as skating, have only
thickened the fog.

Waxing need not be mysterious or difficult. It can be as simple as
you wish. But just as enjoying cross-country skiing requires learning
some technique, mastering waxing calls for a few simple routines. To
wax well, all you need to know is how wax works in general, how much
of it you need, and how to use it. No more. It's that easy. The only
waxing problem is that waxing is often overrated.

ON SNOW

All skiing—be it cross-country skiing, Alpine skiing, ski jumping,
Telemark skiing, or any mongrel form of the sport—involves skis
moving on snow. That's basic.

And ski movement on snow involves glide or changes of glide. The
changes can be changes of direction, as in downhill ski turns. Or they
may be changes of speed, such as by the propulsive kicks of cross-
country ski strides. So all skiing is gliding, more or less. Controlling
that gliding is the essence of ski technique, and of waxing and caring
for skis.

Snow scientists have many theories to explain why skis glide on
snow. Most are complex, and none is exactly right all the time. But the
simplest, most straightforward explanation is correct enough for most
skiing: a ski melts the underlying snow surface particles just enough to
provide an ultrathin layer of moisture on which the ski glides.

When the same ski is waxed, motionless and weighted, as in the kick of the cross-country diagonal stride, the small irregularities in the snow surface don't melt, but dig into the wax, providing grip. The art of waxing for cross-country strides focuses on controlling ski grip and glide on snow.

A well-waxed ski glides on moisture. A stationary, weighted ski can grip the snow, giving a platform for a propulsive kick.

There would be no art to learn if snow were straightforward stuff. It isn't. Its unpredictability is due to its being made up of tiny, hard, sharp crystals of frozen water. The hardness and sharpness of these crystals determine snow properties.

At temperatures well below freezing, all the water in the snow is frozen. The snow is said to be *dry*. The lower the temperature, the dryer and harder the snow crystals. At temperatures above freezing, the snow crystals start to melt. The snow is said to be *wet*. The higher the temperature, the wetter and softer the snow crystals. As fallen snow gets old, it settles, rounding off the crystals. Snow can melt and refreeze, which turns the crystals into larger grains, or "corns," of ice. So snow can vary from heavy and dense to light and fluffy. It can blow like dust, flow like grease, or harden into clumps. It can be moderately cold, like refrigerated food, or extremely cold, like things stored in a deepfreeze. It can be sopping wet, like watery oatmeal, or seemingly as dry as desert sand. Along with these differences go changing properties that affect ski glide and grip. And because no one material, no one wax changes like snow, there are many waxes. The only tricky part of waxing is judging snow so you can select and apply the correct wax.

First waxing rule:
Don't think straight. Snow doesn't act that way. In all waxing, let snow call the shots.

Grip is the secret of the diagonal stride on the flat

You need more grip to diagonal stride uphill

Downhills test glide

You need both grip and glide in the uphill herringbone

THE WAYS TO GO

The best approach to waxing is to wax according to your skiing needs.
Do you, for instance:
Ski infrequently, for recreation?
Ski frequently and far, piling up many miles per season?
Race or otherwise seek maximum performance?
And do you ski:
Anywhere, often in untracked snow?
Only at cross-country areas on machine-prepared trails?
Answers to these questions are your guide to the waxing best suited to
your skiing needs.

Second waxing rule:
Keep it simple. Spend your time skiing, not waxing.

If you are just taking up cross-country skiing, are a more experienced recreational skier who skis infrequently, or ski for utilitarian reasons, such as oversnow backpacking, you are one of the true classical cross-country skiers. You will ski and enjoy skiing wherever you find snow. Waxing ease is important; you can ski a lot with just two waxes, one for dryer snows below freezing and one for wetter snows above freezing. You should opt for a *two-wax* approach, *even if you have waxless skis.*

If you're an avid cross-country skier, a citizens' racer, or devoted wilderness skier, then you probably are willing to sacrifice some convenience for better performance. *Selected waxing* is your approach; you'll use four or five waxes suited to the snows where you ski.

If speed is your game, ski performance is your goal. Each time you ski, you seek the ultimate, the best match of ski to snow. Whether you elect classical cross-country skiing or skating, *performance waxing* is your approach.

Summing it up, there are four sensible approaches to waxing:

Simple: two waxes for waxable skis or two compounds for waxless skis, plus a scraper-cork, for pleasure skiing on all snows.

Selected: four or five waxes and a few extra waxing tools, for better performance in frequent skiing on all snows.

Performance, classical cross-country: the maximum spectrum of cross-country waxes and waxing aids, for best performance in track skiing; mostly for expert skiers and racers.

Performance, skating: skating waxes, waxing aids, and ski base grooming tools, for best performance in skating on prepared courses; mostly for expert skiers and racers.

Two-wax system

Four-wax system

Complete: the whole works for racers/experts

ABOUT WAX

Ski wax is seldom just wax; there are a variety of products for waxing skis:

Grip waxes for classical cross-country skiing divide into *hard* waxes for new or slightly settled snow, usually at or below freezing, and *klister,* for snow that has melted and refrozen. There's also a hybrid *klisterwax,* a cross of the two major types. Hard waxes come in small metal-foil containers. Klister usually comes in tubes, like toothpaste, or in pressurized cans like shaving cream.

Glide waxes are used together with grip waxes, and are applied to tip and tail sections of ski bases to increase glide. They come in small metal-foil containers as do hard grip waxes, or in longer wax rods.

Skating waxes are used over the entire ski base, for glide only. They come in small blocks, so different waxes may easily be melted and mixed to suit snow conditions.

Cleaners are solvents used to remove wax. They come in cans, and where legal, in aerosol sprays.

BE SNOW WISE

Judging snow is the first and most important step in all waxing. Temperature is a good guide. If the snow-level air temperature is well below freezing, −4° C (25° F) or below, almost all the water in the snow is frozen and the snow is *dry*. If it's well above freezing, +1° C (34° F) or above, the snow usually contains liquid water; it's *wet*.

Temperatures shown on outdoor thermometers can mislead, especially if the thermometers are mounted high above the snow or are exposed to the sun. Also, new snow often may be colder or warmer than the air temperature just above the snow surface. So always think of temperature as the first, but not only, guide to selecting wax.

Use wall-mounted thermometers only as a guide; they can mislead.

One of the best ways to check snow type is by squeezing a handful of it in your gloved hand. If the snow is loose and powdery or blows away when you open your hand, it's dry. If it forms snowballs or large clumps, it's wet. Learning to judge the wetness of snow, by observing temperature and feeling the snow, is one of the greater skills in waxing. Waxmakers compound their products for snow types and temperature ranges; if you can judge snow, you can wax. Practice makes perfect.

Squeeze a handful of snow.

If it blows away when you open your hand, it's dry.

If it forms a snowball, it's wet.

If the snowball wets your hand and drips, it's sopping wet.

Third waxing rule:
Get to know snow. That's what makes waxing easy.

PUTTING IT ON

Wax indoors whenever possible. It's more comfortable than standing
outside, and wax goes onto and sticks better to skis when both wax and
skis are at indoor temperatures.

Fourth waxing rule:
Do it indoors if you can.

Always start with clean, dry skis. Wax doesn't stick to dirt or
water. If your skis are waxed incorrectly for the day's snow, remove
the old wax and clean bases before rewaxing.

Hard waxes: All dry-snow waxes and some wet-snow waxes of
two-wax systems come in foil cans, so start by peeling off a strip of foil
to expose the wax. Apply the wax in short, rapid strokes, crayoning it
onto the base. Cover the entire base. You don't need to wax the
tracking groove in the center of the base, as wax may fill the groove,
causing the ski to yaw, or "swim" when gliding. Rub the wax out with
a waxing cork.

Opening wax can

Applying hard wax

The lower the temperature, the smoother the wax should be. For
temperatures of $-4°$ C ($25°$ F) and below, cork the wax out to a shine.
For warmer snows, at temperatures closer to freezing, you need not
polish the wax to a shine, but you should smooth out any clumps as
they might slow glide. When in doubt, wax thin, and add layers if you
need more grip when skiing. More layers give better ski grip, while
fewer, thinner layers give better ski glide.

Corking out hard wax

Opening klister tube

Klisters are tacky, thick liquids. Beware; they can be tricky if handled unskillfully; they can stick to hands, clothes, equipment—anything. But treat them with respect, and they'll behave beautifully. Klisters must be applied warm. When cold, you cannot coax them out of their tubes, not even with brute force. Start by piercing a hole in the ferrule to open the tube; caps have a sharp point for this purpose. If the klister refuses to flow when you squeeze the tube, warm the tube slightly, over a radiator or in your hand. Then squeeze out klister onto the ski base. Some skiers prefer to squeeze out longer, straight strips, while others prefer short diagonal stripes. Smooth out the klister with the spreader paddle packed with the tube. Some skiers like to spread klister and work it into the ski base using the base of their palm. If you don't mind the sticky approach, it is an excellent way to get the job done.

Applying klister in two strips   **Spreading klister applied in two strips**

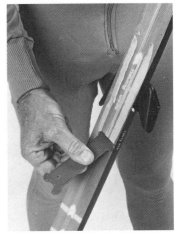

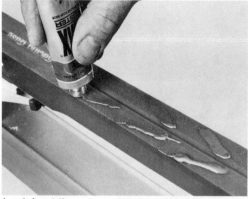

Applying klister in small diagonal strips

Spreading diagonal strips of klister

Applying spray klister

Fifth waxing rule:
Less is best. More not only costs more; it works worse.

There's a one-word rule for applying klisters: *Thin!* Apply klister about as thick as a coat of paint, no more. As soon as you've finished squeezing klister onto your ski bases, put the cap back on the tube. This simple step spares you the mess that critics contend is klister's disadvantage. Klister can continue to flow after you have squeezed the tube, not to mention what might happen if you drop the tube on the floor and then step on it. Avoid these problems and you'll become a klister fan. Klisters invariably grip better than hard waxes; if you have the right klister, you're almost assured good traction. On the snows for which it's intended, nothing can beat it. Just ask any Australian skier.

Klister-waxes come in cans like hard wax, but behave more like klisters. If in doubt, check: dab a fingertip on top of the wax. If it sticks in tacky strings when you pull your finger off, it's a klister-wax, or a sibling requiring like treatment. Start applying klister-wax like hard wax, by peeling off a bit of the container. But don't crayon it on, as rubbing may cause it to come off on the ski base in unmanageable clumps. Instead, dab the wax against the ski base at intervals about equal to the diameter of the wax can. Rub the dabbed-on wax smooth with a waxing cork—or, if you don't mind sticky palms, with the base of your hand. As with klister: thin!

Glide waxes and skating waxes are close cousins to the waxes used in Alpine skiing and ski jumping. Applying them properly entails heating, cooling, scraping, and buffing. Their use is part of performance waxing.

TAKING IT OFF

Like waxing, cleaning skis is best done indoors. Always clean skis before applying new wax, working on bases, or storing skis. Most ski waxes harden on skis stored at room temperature for a few days, so if you are a weekend skier, it's best to clean your skis well after a weekend of skiing. If you drive with skis exposed on an auto roof rack, be sure to clean your skis after taking them off the rack, as road films, dusts, and salt are notorious destroyers of plastic ski bases.

Start cleaning skis using a ski scraper to remove as much old wax as possible. Some skiers find broad-bladed putty knives handy for the job, while others use the klister spreader paddles packed with klister tubes. Be careful when using metal scrapers on plastic bases, as metal edges can dig into and damage base plastic. After you have removed

**Better yet, fix ski horizontal
to scrape off wax**

**Hold ski diagonally, tail on
floor, and scrape off wax**

as much old wax as possible with a scraper, use a ski cleaner liquid
and a lint-free rag or wiping tissue to finish the job. Always follow
directions when using cleaning fluids and use them in well-ventilated
places. *Never use lighter fluid, gasoline, or turpentine to clean ski
bases.* These fluids are not only hazardously flammable, but they can
dissolve ski bases.

Scrape off klister   **Finish clean bases**
with smooth sweeps of scraper   **with wax remover and wiping tissue**

WHAT'S WAX?

Ski waxes are blended from various raw materials of differing types and quantities to produce the desired characteristics. Many, such as glide and skating waxes, are true to their name, and are made almost entirely from raw waxes. Some, such as klisters, contain little or no wax. To the snow scientist or linguistic purist, this presents a problem. English, in contradistinction to the Scandinavian languages of the countries where skiing originated, fails to differentiate between *wax*, the general term for a large group of fatty solids, and *ski wax*, what you put on your skis. But it's an inconsistency easy to live with, as no ski wax contains just wax.

The first ski waxes were hand brewed from vegetable and animal compounds, such as tars, beeswax, and spermaceti (used by the 1848 California Gold Rush miners in downhill ski races). An aura of mystery, and often correspondingly mysterious odors, surrounded these brews. Those days are gone forever, as few modern waxes contain any of the oldtime, natural ingredients. The major waxmakers use none at all.

Hard grip waxes consist mostly of various petroleum waxes, obtained from refining oil. As most petroleum waxes are hard and brittle, they are adulterated with oil and petroleum jelly, for softness, and high-molecular synthetic rubber for internal cohesion and adhesion to ski bases.

Klisters consist mostly of synthetic resins and esters. As these raw materials often are hard when cold, they are softened with oils and petroleum jelly. The oil content is a major factor in determining final klister properties. Red Klister, for instance, is intended for wetter snows, and therefore contains more oil than does Blue Klister, intended for icy snows. Synthetic rubbers are added to improve internal cohesion, the property that makes the klister stick to itself and not rub off on snow. Rubber content depends on snow abrasion: klisters for colder, icy snows contain more rubber than klisters for soft, wet snow. Some klisters contain special adulterants for specific properties, such as metal particles in Silver Klister to increase surface hardness and reduce tackiness.

Glider and skating waxes are made from various paraffins and microcrystalline petroleum waxes and various additives. Types differ basically in hardness, which is regulated by choice of the raw petroleum waxes: waxes with low melting points are the softest, while those with high melting points are the hardest.

TWO WAXES—THE FIRST RESORT

Two-wax systems are the ultimately convenient of waxing approaches. The waxes are compounded to suit wide ranges of snow conditions and to go onto skis easily. With only two waxes to keep track of, selection is simple: one for dry snow, one for wet snow.

Start by following the manufacturer's directions, selecting and applying the correct wax for the conditions as you judge them. Wax a thin layer, over the entire length of the ski base. When in doubt, wax for colder, dryer conditions. If you err, your skis will glide well, but grip poorly. It's always easier to add wax for more grip than to scrape skis for more glide. And you can always add softer wax for warmer snow on top of harder wax for colder snow. But the reverse seldom works well, unless you use more advanced waxing techniques (see pp. 28–30). Hard on top of soft is like putting peanut butter on top of jelly on a single slice of bread: it will slide right off.

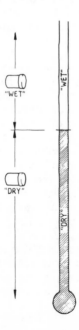

Two waxes are the simplest, one for above freezing, one for below

Sixth waxing rule:
Soft on top of hard. Doing it the other way isn't easy.

Always test your wax by skiing a few hundred yards. If your skis slip totally out of control or ball up with snow before you've taken more than a few strides, then you've missed completely. Go back and start over. Fortunately such drastic misses are seldom; the wide-range waxes of two-wax systems are kind to the skier, which is why they have been used on major ski expeditions.

If you need more grip, add another layer of wax, thickest in the middle of the ski base. Rub out each layer of wax. If you need more glide, try polishing your wax more with a cork. If that fails, remove a bit of wax, especially that under the front and rear thirds of the ski base. If you still lack glide, then you've probably applied the "wet" wax on a day that calls for "dry." Scrape the "wet" wax off, reapply the "dry," and you'll probably glide well.

Experiment with your two waxes and learn to use them for the conditions you most often ski. If another skier waxes better with another brand, you may or may not be equally lucky if you switch to that brand. Most waxing difficulties are caused by improper wax selection or application, not by particular brand choice. In other words, select one brand that is available where you live or where you ski, and get to know it well.

Seventh waxing rule:
One brand is enough. Two make waxing twice as difficult.

Universal wide-range waxes

TWO FOR WAXLESS, TOO

Waxless skis don't need wax for grip and glide. But they do need care for good grip and glide. Their bases are made of the same plastics as are waxable ski bases, and unprotected plastics wear, oxidize, and pick up dirt from snow, all of which degrade ski performance.

Products for retarding wear and retaining waxless ski base performance divide into waxes applied to the tip and tail glide sections of the base, and waxes or liquids applied or sprayed onto the center waxless grip section. The glide waxes are rubbed on and may be corked out as are hard cross-country waxes for cold snows. Grip waxes for waxing pattern bases are rubbed on, and liquids or sprays for waxless composite material bases are brushed or sprayed on.

Preparations for waxless skis

SELECT FOUR OR FIVE

If you want improved performance on snows beyond that afforded by the two-wax approach, you'll want to broaden your range of waxes and waxing techniques. As you still may ski anywhere there is snow, classical cross-country, the sport for all snows, is still your form of skiing.

Here you can learn from waxmakers' sales figures: four or five waxes always account for over 90% of the cross-country wax sold. The exact four or five types vary by region: skiers in the interior of Alaska use more cold-snow hard wax, and skiers in the wetter snows of the Pacific Northwest use more klisters. The lesson is clear: you need no more than four or five waxes to wax well for skiing in your region. If you travel to other skiing climates, you may need other waxes—but still usually no more than four or five total.

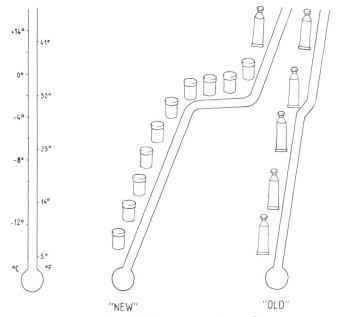

°C °F   "NEW"   "OLD"

For performance matching of skis to snow, you need many waxes, more hard waxes than klisters because new snow properties change most radically at freezing.

If you need more grip on uphill stretches in wet snows, it's time to think of adding klisters. If you need more glide in cold snows well below freezing, then it's time for colder hard waxes. If you ski long tours, or if you ski on icy, abrasive snows, or both, you may find your wax wears quickly. That's a signal to get involved with heat in applying waxes, and to add a base wax, or binder, to your collection.

Heat is the easiest way to increase wax durability. Apply the first layer, and warm it onto the ski, to bond it to the ski base. The most frequently used tool for the job is also the most readily available: an inexpensive travel iron. Most wax makers offer rectangular aluminum irons, with insulated handles, designed for heating with a torch flame, and some offer handy iron heads that fit ordinary 80-watt soldering irons that you can buy in hardware stores. Let the warmed-in wax cool at room temperature, and then smooth it out. Apply subsequent layers without heat, so they don't mix with the first layer.

Eighth waxing rule:
Learn a lot about a few waxes. It's more experience, not more waxes, that makes you a better waxer.

ABOUT SKATING

Skating has divided cross-country skiing and waxing into *classical* and *free-style*. *Classical* involves traditional stride techniques and waxing for grip and glide. *Free-style,* the international euphemism for "non-classical," involves skating strides and waxing for glide only.

Just as roller skating on a hard surface is faster than running on the same surface, skating on skis is faster than traditional striding on packed snows. This is why racers developed skating techniques: on modern, machine-packed courses, there's no faster way for trained athletes to get from the start to the finish. But just as you can run but not roller skate on soft turf, traditional cross-country remains the easier and faster technique for snows that aren't packed. So skating doesn't replace classical cross-country skiing, any more than roller skating replaces running. The sports are different.

In May 1986, after a couple of trial seasons and much debate, the FIS (International Ski Federation) officially recognized that difference and accordingly split racing, ruling that the 1987 Obertsdorf World Ski Championships and 1988 Calgary Winter Olympic cross-country events were to be divided. The relays (4 X 5 km for women, 4 X 10 km for men) and longest events (20 km for women, 50 km for men) are freestyle; the middle events (5 and 10 km for women, 15 and 30 km for men) are classical.

As recreational skiing almost always follows racing, skating is now more common in pleasure skiing. There's no doubt about it: skating is fun, and kids are thrilled by it because it's fast. But the drawback of skating is that it's limited to cross-country ski areas, where the tracks are prepared by machines as they are for racing. Also, even though any moderately proficient skier can skate on the flat, only strong, skilled skiers and racers can skate uphill.

So the division actually is between the traditional strides of cross-country skiing, used for going *through* or *on* snow, anywhere, by anyone, and the newer skating strides, used for speed on packed courses, primarily by expert skiers and racers. The two forms of the sport cannot be compared because they differ in purpose and requirements.

In principle, waxing for skating sounds simpler than waxing for classical cross-country: no fuss with those grip waxes, just put paraffin on the whole ski and skate away. But in practice that isn't the case. Just as ice skaters know the importance of sharpening skates, snow skating skiers know that waxing and care of their ski bases is decisive. When ski

glide is the only way to propel yourself on snow, small differences add up to slow you down or tire you more rapidly.
Although skaters deal with fewer waxes than do classical
cross-country skiers, they often spend more time working on
their skis. In terms of wax use, it's a toss up. Even waxmakers
agree to that: Skating waxes cost about the same as waxes for
classical cross-country. Racers, who gobble more wax than
anyone else for classical cross-country, consume even
greater quantities of wax for skating, some 20% more.

Irons are used mostly for warming in hard wax, as ironing in klister
can be a bit messy. One way of avoiding a sticky iron is to warm in
klister with the flame of a waxing torch fitted with a flame spreader.
But use torch flames sparingly, because flame heat can easily damage
bases. The polyethylene plastic used in most bases starts to melt at
$130°$ C $(265°$ F), well below the $175°$ C $(330°$ F) temperatures commonly used in household ovens to bake bread. Use a flame only
enough to cause the klister to flow on a horizontal, upturned ski base,
and keep it moving to avoid overheating the ski base. One way to
avoid flame damage is to avoid flame by using other heat sources to
warm in klister. One favorite source is an inexpensive or discarded
hair dryer. You would have to deliberately work to damage a ski base
with the heat a hair dryer puts out.

Ninth waxing rule:

Be kind to your bases. They may look tough, but they need tender loving
care.

For icy, abrasive snows, bond wax to ski bases with base wax, or
base binder. Start with a clean, dry ski base, as binder doesn't stick on
top of other wax. It's the tackiest of all waxes that come in cans, as its
purpose is only to bond, not to grip or glide on snow. Treat binder with
more caution than klister-wax, dabbing it on carefully in small
amounts. If the binder sticks to the base only in unruly clumps, try
cooling the can outside before application. Cold binder can be
crayoned on warm bases, just as if it were hard wax. Use a warm
waxing iron to spread, warm, and smooth the binder to an ultrathin,
even layer on the base. Let the skis cool to room temperature, and then
set them outside to cool for a while. Give cooled binder a rapid polish
with a well-used waxing cork; don't use a new cork, as its surface may
be rough and flake off, leaving cork particles in the sticky binder. Then
wax over the binder for the day's conditions. But don't heat the layers

applied on top of the binder. Heat causes the binder to work up into the wax, which may drastically slow ski glide, as raw binder has some grip, but absolutely no glide. You can apply binder over the entire length of a ski base, if you final wax the entire base. But the easiest method is to apply binder over the center third of the base, which is most critical for grip.

The diagonal stride is the backbone of classical cross-country ski racing (racer: Brit Pettersen)

PERFORMANCE CROSS-COUNTRY WAXING

The gear for classical waxing, plus waxes as needed

Performance waxing of performance skis involves waxing methods that evolved from but differ from those common in recreational skiing. The differences arise partly because more waxes are used to attain the best possible match of ski base to snow, and partly because performance skis have cambers and bases differing from those of recreational skis. The cambers are relatively stiffer, and become more so as they close, in a fashion similar to a multileaf truck spring becoming stiffer as the truck is loaded down. The midsections of the bases contact the snow slightly or not at all when the skis are equally weighted, as in downhill skiing or in gliding after double poling. But when kicked down, as in diagonal striding, the middle of the base is pressed against the underlying snow. The base material, usually a

Mid sections of skis are off the snow in gliding on two skis, but in contact with the snow during kicks on one ski.

sintered high-molecular polyethylene plastic, glides best when waxed with glide waxes. Therefore the middle of the base is most active in grip, and the tip and tail sections of the base are most important in glide. So there are three waxing zones on performance ski bases: a center grip zone, a tip glide zone ahead of the center zone, and a tail glide zone behind it. The flip side of the nature of performance skis is that if you don't have it, there's no sense trying to exploit it. In other words, performance waxing won't work very well on recreational skis.

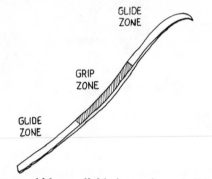

Performance ski bases divide into grip and glide zones.

Tenth waxing rule:
Match waxing to skis. What's underneath wax also counts.

Find the Middle
The bases of most performance skis have marks to indicate the middle grip zone and interval distances from it. If your skis lack these marks, you must locate the mid zone. It isn't in the center of the ski, but rather in the center of the ski camber curve, which is located at different places on different skis. So you must test to find the middle of the camber curve. Ski factories and shops can do this with ski testers. But you can do almost as well by hand.

Hold a pair of skis vertically, bases together, and sight through the gap between the cambers as you squeeze the skis together with your hands just behind the bindings (or for new skis without bindings, at a point just behind the balance point). When the gap closes down to about 75 cm (2½ ft.), mark its front and rear points on the skis. The section of the base between these marks is the center zone.

The exact length of the center zone that you should wax for grip depends on your skis, your proficiency and skiing speed, and on the snow conditions. The general rule is the stickier the grip wax, the less the length of it applied in the center zone. But that rule doesn't give

---

WAXING VIEWS

Many opinions have been voiced on waxing. Here are a selected few.

"Waxing is handicraft."
> Wollzenmuller and Wenger, in *Optimal Waxing of Cross-Country Skis* (in German), 1984.

"Waxing may be a little more complicated than making a peanut-butter-and-jelly sandwich, but the aim is to keep it simple."
> Ned Gillette, in *Cross-Country Skiing*, 1979.

"The best way to view the entire art of waxing is to regard a ski base and ski wax together, as a single unit interacting with snow."
> Waxing scientist Leif Torgersen, in *Good Glide*, 1984.

"I thought cross-country skiing was a gas, until I found out you have to wax the skis every time you go out. Screw it."
> Young dropout from Yosemite School of Ski Touring, as quoted by author Hal Painter in *The Cross-Country Ski, Cook, Look & Pleasure Book*, 1973.

"When everything else has failed, read the instructions. They are printed on the tin or tube in at least three languages."
> Erling Strom describing cross-country skiing in Canada in the 1930s, in *Pioneers on Skis*, 1977.

"Waxing is like foreplay: You can make do without, but it's so much better with."
> Playboy Magazine article *What's New in Cross-Country Skiing*, January 1981.

"The wax question is a deep secret into which it takes years to penetrate."
> *Skiing*, in the *Official Souvenir Book of the III Olympic Winter Games, Lake Placid, New York, February 1932*.

---

you any numbers: you still don't know how many inches of the base to grip wax. Fortunately there's a quick check: wax the entire base with cross-country wax, and then ski about 5 km (3 miles) in abrasive snow tracks. Where the wax has worn off locates the glide zones, and where the wax is still on the skis locates the length of the center grip zone to be waxed for the prevailing conditions.

Prepping First

Always prepare new performance ski bases with glide wax. Reprepare bases whenever the glide zones seem dry or no longer feel soapy to the touch, or whenever they take on a whitish tinge. Base preparation and final glide waxing are nearly identical processes and use similar or sometimes the same glide waxes. The basic difference is that in preparation you work more to bond the glide wax better to the ski base.

Heat makes it possible. Molten paraffin wax and warmed ski base polyethylene plastic actually mix slightly, in a manner chemists call a solution. The base polyethylene plastic itself is not porous, as is often popularily assumed in explanations of its ability to hold wax. If it were, it would also act like a sponge and absorb water. But it doesn't, because polyethylene is *hydrophobic:* it repels water. Heat is the catalyst that brews the paraffin-polyethylene solution, bonding the wax to the ski base.

Start preparing bases with the skis horizontal, bases up, preferably firmly clamped in ski vises or on a waxing horse. Melt the prepping glider onto the skis with an iron, set to 100° to 130° C (212° to 266° F), or *medium* to *high* on ordinary household electric irons. Hold the corner of the iron just above the base, press the wax against the iron so it melts, and drip molten wax down to strips on either side of the tracking groove. Then smooth the wax out with the iron, warming it thoroughly in.

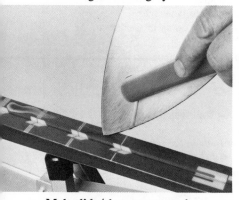

Melt glide/skate wax onto base with warm iron   **Iron wax in**

Apply wax only to the tip and tail glide zones, not to the center grip zone, as cross-country waxes will not stick to but will slide right off glide wax. Applying glide wax in the grip zone makes as much sense as greasing a surface to be painted. In the center zone, cross-country wax warmed in prepares the base as well as can any glide wax.

Let the warm waxed skis cool at room temperature until the wax has hardened, which usually takes 15 to 30 minutes. Then scrape the wax on the base to an ultrasmooth layer, using a rectangular plastic ski scraper. If you feel confident enough, you may use a steel scraper; but be careful, because if you slip when scraping, a steel edge can easily dig a small trench in the base. Scrape the bases until all the prepping glide wax you applied seems to have been removed, and only that which has penetrated into the base material remains. Remove excess wax from the tracking groove with a round, dull object, such as the rounded corner of a klister spreader paddle.

Scrape off excess wax with a rectangular scraper

Remove wax from tracking groove

The Kicker

Apply grip waxes in the center zone, using the same techniques as for recreational waxing (pp. 10–13). As the only purpose of the wax is to grip for kick, you may wax slightly softer than you would in waxing the entire base for recreational skiing under the same conditions. Some racers have skied almost an entire season using only Blue Extra "kickers", even on snows far colder than the range just under freezing for which Blue Extra is intended.

For more grip, increase the length of the kicker, preferably slightly more towards the tip than towards the tail, as the tail glide section is most important in downhill skiing.

Glide Waxing

For glide waxing you may use Alpine ski waxes, but cross-country glide waxes are better, for two reasons. First, they are compounded for maximum durability at lower skiing speeds than are Alpine ski waxes. An Alpine ski race seldom lasts more than a couple of minutes, and speeds are high. A cross-country ski racer is often out for hours, skiing at relatively lower speeds. Second, most waxmakers ease glide wax selection by color-coding their cross-country glide waxes to correspond to the color-coding of the cross-country waxes most frequently used for grip on the same snows. So to select, you match colors.

Apply glide wax in the same way as base preparation wax. For best glide, always scrape glide-waxed zones carefully, and finish the job by polishing smooth with a well-used waxing cork. If you have structured the bases with rill grooves (see pp. 35–36), do *not* polish with a cork, but finish by brushing with a stiff nylon bristle brush to remove wax from the rills.

Action of water drop on ski base indicates glide: better glide if drop stays round; poorer glide if drop spreads.

Beware the overdo in glide waxing. Even skilled skiers and racers often err in seeking glide through endless test skiing and rewaxing of tip and tail glide zones. Remember that glide depends more on how little the grip wax drags than on how well the glide wax glides, even with the most meticulous of zone waxing jobs. So to improve glide, work on the grip wax first. Also, ski glide usually improves as skis are used, so the guy who goes out and buys new skis for a race isn't guaranteed the fastest pair in the race.

Binders

For skiing in abrasive snows, you'll need base binder wax "under" the cross-country grip wax in the *center zone only;* use the same methods as for recreational skiing (pp. 21-22). Do *not* put base binder on the glide zones: it will only slow glide. Here base prepping glide wax is the binder. *Stick under grip, slide under glide.*

One or More

Snow dictates waxing, so no one set of instructions, in a book or on a wax container, can tell you exactly how to wax for all conditions. For top performance, you must continually alter your approach as well as pick your wax for the snow involved. Two handy tricks are using just one wax and combining waxes.

One wax only, over the entire base of the ski, may sound amateurish to racers steeped in the more complex approaches of performance waxing, but often it's a reliable approach for cold snows. Glide on colder snows, $-15°$ C ($5°$ F) and below is poor, so the colder the snow, the less glide wax on ski base tips and tails affects glide. The 1980 Lake Placid Winter Olympic men's 15 km race is a case in point. It was run in cold, new snow. Much to the chagrin of many other racers, who had spent hours glide waxing their skis, Swede Thomas

---

NO CHARTS

In the early renaissance of cross-country skiing, wax tables or charts were included in book presentations of waxing. They told readers that many types of wax were available to suit different snows, and that several waxmakers were in the business, as few shops stocked complete ranges. But there are no such tables or charts in this book, for a number of reasons.

First, the need for them has passed. Waxing is a recognized part of the skiing scene, and a well-advertised part at that. It no longer needs introduction.

Second, waxes have now developed to great degrees of convenience, as the two-wax systems, and sophistication, witness the great ranges of waxes available. So equivalence between brands now means little. Changing application rather than switching brands is the best way to improve deficient waxing.

Third, waxmakers now alter their product lines at least once a season, deleting and adding products, and changing existing products and their packaging. Even the most comprehensive table of waxes, correct at the time of compiling, would be outdated by the time it was read in a book.

Fourth, different waxmakers seldom split their ranges of waxes in the same way: for a particular set of snow conditions where one maker offers three waxes, another may offer four, and vice versa.

Finally, modern understanding of skis on snow has underscored the importance of regarding wax as something that works together with a ski base, not just something that is put on top of a base. The *how* is as important as the *what,* so there's no need for a table of *whats.*

Wassberg waxed quickly, with no glide wax at all. He simply put on hard cross-country wax for cold, dry snow, on the entire length of his ski bases. And he won the race. More modern base grooming has outdated Wassberg's trick, but it still has value, especially if you have to wax fast or if you use skis not groomed for cold snows.

One of the more vexing but also more common of tricky racing waxing conditions is hard tracks in older, wetter snow, with a dusting of lighter, new powder snow on top. Tracks often are set in the afternoon or evening for an early-morning race, and powder snow frequently falls in the early morning, producing the condition. If you use klister for the wetter tracks, it will collect the new snow and ice up, at best slowing your glide. If you wax for the new powder alone, you may manage if the race is short, 5 km or less. But over longer distances, the abrasive, older snow in the tracks will scrape off your hard wax. So compromise: apply both klister for the hard tracks and hard wax for the powder. Start with the klister, selecting and applying it just as if the powder weren't there. Then cool your skis outside for half an hour or so. Select the hard wax that you would use on the powder, just as if the older snow weren't there. Apply it sparingly, covering the klister, and smoothing it out with a feathery touch of a waxing cork. This is the reverse of the general rule that hard wax shouldn't be put on top of softer wax. Cooling is the trick that permits it, and for the situation you face, it's about the only thing that works.

For Freezing Slop, Abrade

Waxing for freezing slop—wet new snow or snow mixed with rain, sleet or mist just at freezing, 0° C (32° F)—is difficult, as snow characteristics are unstable, and softer waxes and klisters frequently ice up. One workable approach is to abrade, or selectively roughen base mid sections. The roughening raises small polyethylene fibers up from the base. On the right snow conditions, each fiber acts like a small sawtooth, biting into the snow for grip. Abrading works only over a very narrow range of snow conditions, and it's tough on skis, as some of the base is removed each time it's done. But for classical cross-country ski racing in freezing slop, few wax jobs can beat it. It's

Abrade mid base zone with a rasp

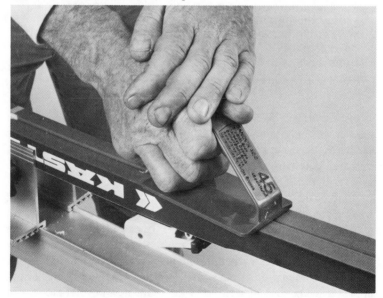

a *Made in USA* technique, originated by US Ski Team racers during the 1981–82 season.

Abrading works best on sintered polyethylene racing ski bases. Extruded plastic bases, common on recreational cross-country skis, black polyethylene containing graphite, and some performance cross-linked polyethylenes are poor performers when abraded. The ideal ski camber for abrading is slightly stiffer than a dry-snow, or "powder" ski camber, but not quite as stiff as a klister ski camber. Few racers enjoy the luxury of a special pair of skis for abrading, so most use an old pair of klister skis.

Start abrading with skis firmly fixed in vises or on a waxing horse or stand, bases completely clean. Tip and tail glide sections may be glide waxed before or after abrading. For abrading use a rectangular, flat rasp fitted to a handle, of the type offered by carpentry toolmakers and some waxmakers. Select a coarser grit, #50, for rougher abrading, and a finer grit, #160, for smoother abrading. Snow conditions determine the grit used: #50 for tracks that pack and polish to a glaze, and #160 for continuously falling new snow.

Abrade base center sections in the tip-to-tail direction, over a length about equal to that where you normally would apply wet snow klister, about 30 to 50 cm. (12 to 20 in.). Abrade until the center section looks as if it were made of fine fur. When in doubt, abrade too little rather than too much, as excessive abrading slows glide.

After abrading, brush and wipe off all abrading dust. Raw abraded bases will ice up if used directly, so wipe or spray on silicone liquid for protection and glide. Waxmakers offer special liquids for this purpose, and sprays intended for protecting composite material

Apply silicone liquid

waxless ski bases also work well. Let the skis stand until the silicone liquid is completely dry.

Like waxless ski bases, abraded ski bases are a fixed, mechanical way to attain grip. Once on skis, you cannot change grip without going back inside to redo the job. So always try abrading in training before using it in racing.

GROOMING BASES

You don't have to race for long to have had another racer glide past you on the flat or zip past you on a downhill. It can happen even if you're identically waxed, so why was your rival faster? Part of the reason may be choice of skis for the snow involved, but most differences in glide are due to differences in bases. Although you wax for glide, it isn't the wax alone that glides; it's the *waxed base surface* that glides. The character of the base surface is vital in determining that glide. So grooming bases to control their surfaces is an important part of performance waxing, both in glide waxing tip and tail zones for classical cross-country and in glide waxing for skating. Bases are groomed to *flat* and to *structure* their surfaces.

Flatting: Ski bases glide best when they are flat, without high or low spots that drag on the snow. But skis can wear unevenly and base shape can change with ski age. Even new ski bases are not always flat, as factory base finish grinding/sanding often is not good enough for racing.

Structuring: Absolutely smooth ski bases often glide poorly; skis seem to stick to snow like two smooth panes of glass sticking to each other. Glide is improved if ski bases have a structure of small grooves to break the suction.

All grooming puts force on the base, so start work with skis firmly fixed in waxing vises or on a waxing horse or stand, bases up. For both new and old skis, first clean the bases thoroughly, using wax remover and wiping tissue.

Flatting

First, check base flatness by sighting under a straight edge placed across the base at several points along the ski. A new metal scraper edge is fine for the purpose.

With sanding paper firmly held in a sanding block, sand bases from tip towards tail, removing any high points found in sighting. Recheck flatness as you sand. Start with grit #100 paper, and finish with grit #180 when the bases appear flat. If you are skilled with tools, you may prefer to use a sharp steel scraper to remove high

Sand bases smooth

points and true bases. Always follow scraping with some sanding. Finally, buff with wiping tissue to remove sanding dust and small threads of base material. For rapid final cleaning, try alternating buffing and brushing with a brass brush. Always wax newly flatted bases as soon as possible, to preserve the job you've done.

Repeat flatting whenever bases wear unevenly or when they acquire a whitish tinge, the sign of advancing oxidation.

A bronze brush quickly removes sanding dust

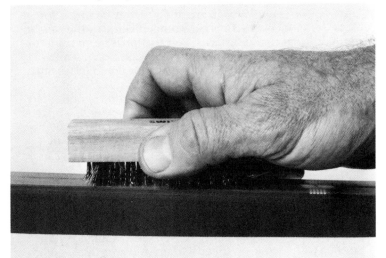

HOW MUCH GRIP, HOW MUCH GLIDE?

Most skiers consciously or unconsciously rate the grip and glide of their skis, sometimes with adjectives unfit for print.

Both grip and glide depend on a ski's resistance to sliding on a snow surface. This resistance is caused by air resistance, displacement of snow (plowing up of snow as the ski moves), and friction. Air resistance and snow displacement are familiar from other activities, which may be why they are so frequently discussed by skiers. But they actually are of lesser importance at cross-country skiing speeds. Friction is more important, but also more subtle and complex in determining overall ski grip and glide.

Friction (from the Latin *fricare,* to rub) occurs whenever two surfaces contact each other. It's inescapable, and it's both friend and foe. You couldn't walk without it. You use it when you write, depend on it when you strike a match. But lack of it can cause cars to skid and wheels to spin.

In cross-country stride techniques, you need friction for grip. And although it opposes and therefore limits ski glide, you wouldn't want to do away with friction completely. If you did, you couldn't turn or control your skis on the underlying snow, or even get underway.

Almost everything that can be said about friction can be expressed in terms of the *friction coefficient.* The two main types of friction coefficient are *dry* and *wet.* The dry friction coefficient is the sort explained in high-school science classes, the type you encounter in sliding furniture across floors, or in everyday walking. It's just the frictional force along the surfaces touching each other divided by the weight perpendicular to the surfaces. Wet friction is more complex and less well understood, as it depends also on the areas in contact and on the viscosity of the wetting liquid (viscosity is a liquid's internal resistance to flow). Snow researchers know that neither dry friction nor wet friction completely describes ski grip or glide. Something in between, a mixed friction, is involved. As yet, nobody is certain about the "laws" of mixed friction. But you can simplify a view of it if you think of the old standby dry friction coefficient as a guideline.

Just how much or how little should the friction coefficient be for good ski grip and glide? The numbers alone have little meaning; it's their result, how they affect your skiing, that counts. Think, for instance, of the caveats in state driver's manuals and safety campaigns: vehicle stopping distance goes up with increased speed and up still more on wet or icy roads.

The friction coefficient between good car tires and dry pavement is about 0.8, which limits vehicle braking distance at the Interstate limit of 55 m.p.h. to a minimum of 127 feet on a level road. Actual stopping distance is, of course, greater, as even the best brakes waste some stopping energy, and driver reaction distance adds to the total.

If the same road is wet, the friction coefficient drops to 0.5, which ups the minimum braking distance at 55 m.p.h. from 127 to 203 ft. An icy road, with a tire-to-road friction coefficient of 0.1, will further increase the minimum braking distance to 1020 ft.

In normal walking, you need a friction coefficient of 0.2 or more between your feet and the underlying surface. If that friction coefficient drops to 0.1, you instinctively slow down, feel uneasy, and take shorter strides.

For gliding skis, a friction coefficient of 0.1 is moderate to poor; one of 0.05 is good. To see the difference, think of zipping downhill at 25 m.p.h. and coasting out onto a flat in even, level tracks. With a friction coefficient of 0.1, you'll stop in 210 ft. With a friction coefficient of 0.05, you'll coast 420 ft. before stopping. For grip, you don't need much friction: a friction coefficient of 0.4 to 0.5 is usually adequate. What's slippery for a car on a wet road is good snow bite for a cross-country ski kick.

Structuring

Structuring involves producing longitudinal patterns in bases for best glide on the snow involved. In general, the older and wetter the snow, the rougher the structure necessary: coarse structure for wet klister, medium structure for most snows below freezing, and fine structure for cold snows. For skating, the entire base running surface is structured, while for classical cross-country, only the tip and tail glide zones are structured.

The longitudinal grooves are produced by draw cutting from the tip towards the tail. Sanding paper can be used for this purpose: #100–#150 grits for wet snow and slush, #150–#180 grits for average snows, −10° to +2° C (14° to 36° F), and #220–#320 grits for cold snows, −10° C (14° F) and below. But sanding requires skill in drawing the sanding paper evenly along the base of the ski to produce the desired rill structure. So waxmakers now offer *rillers*, special

Small, parallel rills in bases can promote glide only if brushed clean of excess wax.

planes with interchangeable blades, that ease and speed structuring. To use a riller, follow manufacturer's directions to select the blade to suit the snow, and push the riller along the ski base, from tip to tail. Use firm pressure and long, even strokes.

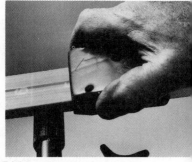

Rill bases with even strokes

Riller has interchangeable blades
to suit different snows

After sanding or rilling, always buff bases with wiping tissue to remove burrs and sharp edges on the rills. Prep wax newly structured bases as soon as possible. Warm in glide wax or skating wax in the usual way, and let it cool and harden. Scrape off excess hardened wax with light strokes of a plastic scraper. Do not use a metal scraper for this purpose, as its sharp blade can damage the rill structure. Finally, brush excess hardened wax out of the rills using a stiff-bristle nylon brush.

Repeat structuring whenever bases are worn smooth or begin to oxidize.

Finally, brush base with a nylon brush

WATCH WEATHER

Temperatures past and present are dominant in determining snow characteristics, but other aspects of weather also influence snow. Here are some that experienced waxers take into account.

Altitude affects waxing. But the effects are indirect, as elevation itself has little influence on snow character. More important is the source of the moisture from which the snow was formed. Snow falling on lower, coastal areas often comes from moisture evaporated from seawater, and may contain traces of salt and other impurities. Snow falling on high, inland mountain areas often comes from moisture evaporated from fresh water, and is purer. Dust, soot, and other contaminants in evaporated moisture also affect the characteristics of snow. Usually there are greater differences in skiing at the same altitude in different parts of the country than in skiing at different altitudes in one region.

Fog soaks. Fog or high air humidity makes snow wetter than it otherwise would be at the same temperature. All ski waxes are compounded for average wintertime humidities, 60% to 70%, so when the humidity is unusually high, or when you ski high in the clouds or in fog, you should wax "warmer." Humidity affects new snow the most and older snow the least, so for klister conditions, humidity has little effect on waxing.

Sun heats. Solar heat melts snow, raising its water content. For tours in sun-drenched snows, you'll have to wax "warmer" than you would for the same snow at the same temperature on an overcast day.

Wind packs. Wind-packed snow acts dryer and harder than it otherwise would be at the same temperature. For wind-pack, wax harder, for colder/older snow than you would for the same snow were it not packed.

Clouds count. Clouds shield the earth from the heat of the sun. But clouds also slow the escape of heat from the earth to space, which is why clear nights usually are colder than cloudy nights. This reverse effect of cloud cover or lack of it affects waxing in two ways. First, after a clear night, snow temperature can be lower than air temperature for several hours, particularly in midwinter when the sun is low in the sky. So after a clear night, wax "cold." Second, on a sunny day, sudden overcasts don't lower snow temperature; they raise it, because the clouds prevent heat escape from the snow. The differences are small, but enough to ruin racer wax tests made when cloud cover shifts.

Exposures differ. Everyone who lives in the snow belt in the Northern Hemisphere knows that the sun melts snow faster on southern than on northern exposures. (The reverse is true in the Southern Hemisphere). That effect on waxing is obvious: snow in the sun is wetter than snow in the shade. But there's also a hidden effect on snows that get little or no sun. On a clear day, they can lose heat rapidly. This means that although morning air temperatures can rise as surrounding air masses are heated by the sun, snow temperature can remain constantly colder, which calls for "colder" waxing.

PERFORMANCE SKATING WAXING

Skating has long been used in cross-country ski racing, particularly on hard, level snow surfaces, such as where courses cross frozen lakes. So skiers may skate flatter stretches with any skis and any good waxing for the conditions involved. But skating an entire race is another matter. To be successful, it requires special skis and special waxing.

Skating skis are usually 10 to 20 cm shorter than classical cross-country ski racing skis, and have cambers designed for ultimate glide.

The gear for skating waxing, plus waxes as needed

Like the bases of classical cross-country skis, the bases of skating skis are made of various compoundings of sintered polyethylene, including material blends, such as those used in black graphite bases.

Although skating avoids classical cross-country's vexing problem of how to wax for the critical transition snows just at freezing, good skating waxing still requires equally careful wax selection and meticulous application. To see why this is so, think of Alpine ski racing, where small differences in ski glide can add up to hundredths or tenths of seconds in results. This is one reason why top Alpine racers are backed by service teams, who often spend hours testing and preparing skis before a race. In cross-country ski skating races, a fraction of an inch less in each gliding stride spells lower speed and/or greater racer

The racing marathon skate is used in tracks (racer: Anette Böe)

Pure skating is used on courses without tracks (racer: Thomas Eriksson)

fatigue, and can add up to minutes in a race. Waxing is a crucial part of skating racing.

Groom First

Skating waxing starts with grooming and cleaning, followed by preparation. Groom and prepare skis firmly clamped in ski vises or on a waxing horse or bench, bases up. Use a base preparation glide wax, melting it onto the skis with an iron, set to 100° to 130° C (212° to 266° F). Hold the corner of the iron just above the base, press the wax against the iron so it melts, and drip molten wax down to strips on either side of the tracking groove. Then smooth the wax out with the iron, warming it thoroughly. Keep moving the iron back and forth until it moves freely in the molten wax.

Allow the wax to cool and harden, which usually takes 15 to 30 minutes. Then scrape off excess wax with a plastic scraper, being careful not to damage any rills structured into the base. Then remove excess wax down in the rills using a stiff-bristle nylon brush. Use a feather touch on the last pass with the brush, to remove any small wax particles left in the rills.

Select, Mix and Apply

Wax selection for skating is like wax selection for classical cross-country: there are many choices. In fact, so great is the demand for "fine tuning" in skating races that glide must be more carefully matched to snow than in classical cross-country; after all, glide is a skating skier's only way to move. Therefore waxmakers offer ranges of three to five skating waxes, to be used individually or mixed according to tables, to match various snows. This is similar to the situation in Alpine ski racing, but because cross-country skating speeds are lower, race durations longer, and underski pressure greater than in Alpine skiing, skating waxes differ from Alpine ski waxes.

Electric waxers, irons fitted with reservoirs and dispensers, are the best tools for melting, mixing and applying skating waxes. But the oldtime ski racer's standby, a small pot on an electric hotplate or Primus stove for melting and mixing, also works well.

Final wax the same way you prep wax, by melting on, smoothing out, cooling, scraping, and brushing. Brushing is the last step; don't follow it with buffing or corking, as rubbing would degrade the waxed structured base surface you've worked to attain.

Waxing can be fun

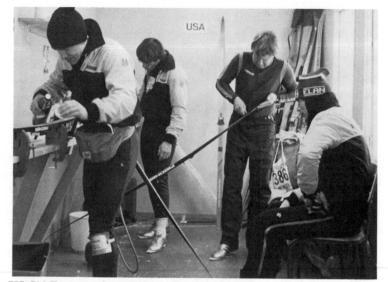

US Ski Team waxing, photo by Michael Brady

WAXING AIDS

Ski Scrapers are available in two basic types: smaller scrapers, often combined with a cork into a single unit, for removing wax and scraping bases, and larger steel or plastic scrapers, about the size of a small filing card, used for scraping and repairing bases and for scraping base preparation wax and glide and skating waxes. One popular steel scraper is an ordinary 3 × 5 inch carpenter's refinishing scraper, available in hardware stores.

Corks, as the name implies, were originally made only of natural cork. Synthetic waxing corks, made of expanded plastics, are now more common, and often better for the job than natural cork.

Thermometers: Ski areas often wall-mount larger, dial-face thermometers, with circular scales in degrees Celsius and degrees Fahrenheit, and sometimes with scales to aid wax selection. Skiers find pocket-type waxing thermometers more handy, as they are not only conveniently small, but can be used to take snow or air temperatures.

Waxing irons are usually small and light, and are available in a variety of designs. Most common are solid rectangular blocks fitted with insulated handles, intended for heating with waxing torches. Electric waxing irons, and waxing-iron attachments for ordinary soldering irons, are also available, while some skiers simply use a small electric travel iron.

WAX WITH WILE

Learn Celsius, or Centigrade temperatures. They're far more convenient for waxing than Fahrenheit temperatures: minus means dry snow, plus means wet snow, and zero is border-line.

Wax cold for a tour in variable snow conditions. If your skis slip on a wet stretch, you double pole or skate to keep moving. But if you've waxed too warm for the dry stretches, your skis may collect snow and ice up. Then you're stuck; you'll have to stop, scrape, and rewax. Anticipate and avoid.

Wax warm for more grip in powder snow. Even if you've waxed correctly for the prevailing temperature and snow type, your skis may slip if you ski untracked powder snow. The loose powder isn't firm enough to withstand the pressure needed for ski grip. Think of sand: sand strewn on an icy road or sidewalk gives you underfoot traction for driving and walking, but driving or walking in loose, dry sand is difficult. So wax as if the temperature were higher.

Change seldom. If yesterday's hard wax still works, leave it on and get more skiing out of it. But it's best to rewax when using klisters or klister-waxes, as they pick up dirt, dust, pine needles, and other wax from snow as you ski.

For glide, think grip. The glide in all classical stride tech-niques depends primarily on how much grip wax drags, and only secondarily on how well any glide wax slides. At best, glide waxes are a five-percent solution; you can easily do without them, unless you are into racing.

Cork, klister paddle, thermometer

Tracks can be cold and rough. Machine-prepared tracks are harder and flatter than tracks set by skiers. So for skiing in tracks, you usually can get away with waxing "colder" for better glide than you would have in skiing outside the tracks in the same snow. Whenever machines set tracks in new snow on top of underlying older snow, some of the older snow gets churned up into the new snow. So in-track snow may differ greatly from out-of-track snow, particularly whenever a thin layer of new powder has fallen on top of a layer of frozen granular snow. The abrasive granular snow particles dug up by the track setter wear wax quickly. For these conditions, you'll need base binder wax.

Artificial snow is different. Man-made snow usually is made from local ground water, which often contains minerals and other impurities. Natural atmospheric snow is almost always more pure. So, just as salt lowers the freezing point of water, turning snow to water on subfreezing roads, minerals in man-made snows make them wetter than natural snows of the same age at the same temperature. So wax warmer on artificial snow.

Check snow. Waxmakers logically state the temperature ranges of their products as still air temperatures slightly above the snow. Few, if any, state snow temperatures. Think: if they did, then how would they state temperatures for use above freezing? The temperature of a snow surface can never go above 0° C (32° F), or it would be water, not snow. But snow temperature does affect waxing, especially early in the morning, when the temperature close to the snow surface hasn't caught up with the sun-warmed air above, or whenever new, cold snow falls during a warmer day. For these conditions, always check snow temperature, using a waxing thermometer; wax according to the temperature you read.

Dry before waxing. Carry a piece of an old terrycloth towel in your wax kit to wipe skis dry before waxing. It's a time saver.

Bag on the road. Carry your skis in a ski bag when traveling, particularly when driving with skis on an auto roof rack. Road film, exhaust particles, and dust dissolve ski base plastics. Worse, saltwater, splashed up from salted roads, etches bindings and skis so quickly that you may suspect the ski industry is among those supporting road salting in skiing states. Best are zippered ski bags, but the disposable plastic bags airlines give away free to bag checked skis or even two overlapped large plastic garbage sacks will do. If your car roof rack is of the locking, hinged type intended to carry skis flat, side by side, best swap it for a simpler roof bar and a couple of rubber or shock-cord tie-downs. Toss the ski bag inside of your car if you fear theft when leaving it unattended.

Electric waxers are irons fitted with a reservoir to hold and melt wax and a dispenser mechanism to spread molten wax on a horizontal upturned ski base. They are especially handy for skating waxing, which involves blending different waxes to match snow conditions for best glide.

Caution: If you travel outside of North America to ski, don't take an electric iron or an electric waxer, unless it is a dual-voltage unit which can be used on 220-volt supplies abroad.

Waxing torches, used for warming in waxes, preparing bases, and cleaning skis, are available in a variety of designs, all fueled with liquefied petroleum gas. The most common types are those fueled by propane cylinders, commonly available in hardware stores, and those fueled by butane cartridges. The propane cylinders are heavier than the lightweight butane cartridges for the same amount of gas, but have the advantage that propane burns well down to $-30°$ C ($-22°$ F), while butane freezes at about $-1°$ C ($30°$ F). The choice between the two depends on whether you are willing to carry a heavier torch that always lights, or opt for a lightweight torch at the expense of having to warm it in your hands or inside clothing so you can light it for use outside in cold weather. *Caution:* If you go overseas to ski, leave your torch behind, and borrow or buy one there. European and North American torch heads are similar, and some are even made by the same companies. But the threads where the gas cylinders and the torch heads mate differ: you can't use a North American torch head on a European gas flask.

Warning: Gas is Grounded

If you fly to ski and take your wax torch along, leave its gas containers behind, as both federal and international aviation safety regulations prohibit their transport on passenger aircraft. The reasons for the restriction are sound: seals on gas-torch refill containers are intended to contain the gas when there's normal air pressure outside and the containers are undamaged. But when outside air pressure drops, as it can in an airplane, or when a container is damaged, as it might be if luggage bounces about, a container can leak, turning an aircraft into a flying bomb. Accordingly, federal regulations are strict: a violation can result in stiff fines and imprisonment. Warnings to this effect are required to be posted by airlines. So if you fly and take your torch, take one that runs on common refills, such as the propane flasks sold in hardware stores throughout the country. The torch-head valve unit is harmless; only the gas is grounded.

Wiping tissue, offered by most major waxmakers, is special lint-free, absorbent tissue, useful in cleaning skis, and buffing bases.

Brushes, small rectangular hand-held brushes with brass bristle for working on bases, and nylon bristle for finishing glide/skating waxing of rill-structured bases.

Hand cleaners, offered by waxmakers, are special creams that will remove wax from hands and clothing. Most mechanic's waterless hand cleaners will also work. Ordinary Vaseline is an acceptable solvent for klisters. Don't use these creams to remove wax from skis, as they leave an oily resideue that repels wax.

Wax removers are liquid solvents offered by waxmakers. They are specially compounded to dissolve wax and evaporate rapidly, yet not damage skis or ski bases. Where legal, they are available in aerosol spray cans for ease of application. *Warning:* Many of these solvents are flammable, and most are harmful if swallowed. If swallowed, do not induce vomiting. Call a physician immediately, Give air to an unconscious patient. Keep solvents out of the reach of children!

Wax kits, as offered by major waxmakers, are plastic cases with hinged sections containing compartments for storing wax and waxing tools. Some skiers prefer to use a sturdy metal fishing-tackle box as a wax kit.

Wax case and tools

Rasps, Rillers, Sanding Paper and Sanding Blocks are all used in grooming ski bases. Rasps are rough metal rectangles fitted to a holder with a handle, and are used by racers for abrading base center sections for grip on troublesome new snows just at the freezing point. Rillers are special base planes that produce small, parallel grooves, or rills (a name borrowed from astronomy) in bases, to promote glide in glide zones of skis performance waxed for classical-cross country and entire bases of skis waxed for skating. Sanding paper for smoothing ski bases isn't ordinary sand paper, but rather cloth- or polyester-backed metal oxide sheets intended for working on plastics; common grits are #150 and #180. Sanding blocks hold sanding paper against a flat surface, with a convenient grip for the hand.

For altering bases (rasp, riller, sandpaper, silicone liquid)

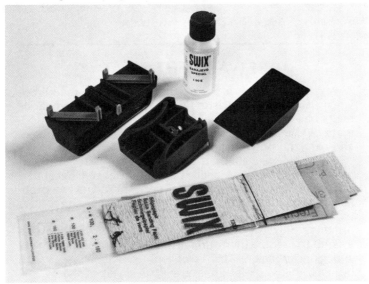

Waxing vises/horses/stands firmly hold skis, bases up. Vises come in pairs, and are clamped to a sturdy table or workbench. Horses resemble a carpenter's horse, and are usually made of metal tubing, collapsable for portability. They stand free on the floor, and hold skis at a convenient level. Stands, or "waxing benches" are available in a variety of designs, some floor standing, some bench/table mounting. One popular model is made of wood, shaped to match the curves and camber of an upside-down ski, with a clamp in the middle to hold the ski down. As the entire ski is supported, it is the best device for heavier work on bases, such as rill structuring.

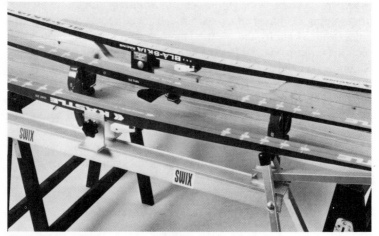

Waxing horse, vises, or bench holds skis stable

BEWARE THE HEAT

Always be at least twice as careful as you think you should be when using heat on plastic ski bases. Extreme overheating melts base polyethylene, which is total destruction. Moderate overheating is more subtle; it oxidizes base surfaces, and oxidized polyethylene glides poorly.

Polyethylene is almost the universal base material on performance skis because it glides well. It glides well because it is hydrophobic: it repels water. This property poses a problem in ski manufacture: ski makers find it difficult to get glues or inks to stick to polyethylene. Therefore, prior to gluing or printing, polyethylene plastic sheets are usually flame treated to oxidize their surfaces, which vastly improves ink and glue adhesion. This is why polyethylene bases with designs, logos, or lettering are actually clear sheets, silk screen printed on the reverse side that is also glued to the body of the ski.

The same oxidation that promotes glue and ink adhesion also permits water absorption, defeating the useful hydrophobic property of polyethylene. Heat from a waxing torch or iron, or even excess sun, can oxidize polyethylene. So caution is the rule. Telltale for oxidation is its color: chalk-white strips or patches signal its advance. If you see oxidation, scrape it off with a steel scraper, and reprep the bases.

SKI CARE AND REPAIR

Clean both waxable and waxless skis after use. Clean skis waxed with klister after each day of skiing. Skis waxed with hard wax or glider/skating wax need not be cleaned as often. Always clean skis that will stand for a few days or more, as wax and dirt on ski plastics hardens with time, and is more difficult to remove when hardened. Clean bases with a scraper and a wax remover solvent, and wipe dry with wiping tissue or lint-free rags. Clean tops and sides with wax remover, with each base cleaning if klister has been used, and whenever they seem to need it if other waxes have been used.

Check binding screws periodically, and tighten whenever necessary, provided the screws are not epoxy bonded in place. Almost all bindings mount with Pozi-Drive #3 screws. Pozi-drive screwdrivers are available from ski shops and some hardware stores. In a pinch, use a Phillips driver, but don't use it much, as its flutes don't match Pozi-drive screws exactly, and it can damage the screws. If the screws are so loose that they turn but don't tighten down, take them out, and plug the holes with plastic plugs (available from ski shops) or homemade wood plugs, set in glue. If your skis have acrylic cores, use epoxy sparingly for this purpose, as it can damage the core material. Re-drill and redrive the screws when the glue has cured.

Repair base damage as soon as possible. First, thoroughly clean the area to be repaired, using wax removing solvent and wiping tissue to remove all foreign matter from a gouge or scrape. Trim away any loose edges. Then, light the end of a polyethylene base-repair "candle" (available from ski shops), and drip molten polyethylene down into the gouge. Let the patch cool for at least 30 minutes, and then scrape off the excess and flatten the base with a steel scraper. Finally, smooth the patch with fine sandpaper. Gouges and scratches in ski sidewalls or tops should also be repaired as soon as possible. Clean the damaged area, and fill with two-component epoxy filler or glue. When the epoxy has hardened, scrape the patch flush with the surrounding surface. Sidewall repairs are more urgent than top repairs, as sidewall damage may permit water to seep into the core of the ski, which can damage internal bonds and weaken the ski.

Delamination is the separation of sandwiched ski layers from each other. It occurs most often at the tail of a ski, but tips also delaminate. First, spread the laminations from each other and block them apart with matchsticks. Clean all surfaces thoroughly with wax remover solvent, and allow the solvent to evaporate completely.

Spread epoxy glue over the most accessible of the surfaces to be joined, remove the matchstick props, and close the laminations together. Apply pressure until the glue cures. C-clamps and blocks are the best way to apply pressure. If you don't have these tools, wrap the ski with strong masking tape, starting with the end of the repair closest to the middle of the ski, and working outwards, squeezing the laminations together and wrapping as you go. When the glue has cured, slit the tape along one ski edge with a knife, and remove it in one big unwrap. Then trim off any surplus glue that oozed out of the joints made.

Warning: Epoxy Hazard

The Public Health Service regards epoxy resins and hardeners as occupational health hazards. You should always observe the safety rules for epoxy use, even if you use only small quantities, such as the two-component epoxy glue or filler for ski repair. In short, the PHS guidelines advise keeping all epoxy materials away from your mouth and eyes, keeping all fire or sparks away from fumes, ventilating well to prevent inhaling vapors, and being meticulous in cleaning up and washing your hands after using epoxy compounds.

Scraper care: Rectangular steel scrapers, used to maintain ski bases, themselves need maintenance, as they dull with use. Dull scrapers are hard to use and can damage skis, as they tend to dig into bases instead of scraping as they should. Keeping a scraper sharp eases scraping. Here's how Stanley Tools, makers of the 3 × 5 inch refinishing scraper available in hardware stores throughout the country, recommends that scrapers be sharpened:

First, clamp the scraper in a vise and file the edges square and straight by draw-filing with a smooth millfile. Round the corners slightly, to prevent their digging in whenever you use the end of an edge. Second, whet the edge, holding the blade vertical, square to the surface of an oil stone. Finally, remove any remaining edge burrs by whetting the scraper flat on the oil stone, smoothing all eight edges so they are sharp.

Storing skis: Always clean skis before storing them for any extended period. Recreational ski plastic bases can be stored with no further treatment, provided they are clean and the skis aren't exposed to high heat in storage. Prepare performance polyethylene bases before storage, by warming in glide wax. Some skiers simply apply the wax in the spring, and scrape in the fall when they take the skis out of storage.

WHAT'S IN A WAX KIT BESIDES WAX

After you have stocked your wax kit with the obvious items— wax, wax removers, waxing tools, cleaner, wiping tissue and the like—you'll probably toss in a few more items to ease waxing and ski care when on the road, away from home. Here's a list of favorite extras carried by avid skiers, racers, and coaches:

Spark lighter: for torch; safer than matches, lessens danger of discarding burning match.

Polyethylene base-repair "candle": for repairing base damage.

Small straight edge: for sighting to check base flatness.

Ski straps: to strap skis together; especially useful when you carry skis with klistered bases.

Plastic lunch bags to put over ski tips and tails for protection when waxed skis are strapped base-to-base for carrying or transporting.

Oil stone: for sharpening metal ski scraper and pole tips.

Epoxy glue: small tubes, for minor ski and pole repairs.

Few extra binding screws.

Pozi-drive no. 3 screwdriver: for tightening binding screws.

Fiberglass tape: for repairing ski poles and, sometimes, skis.

Paint brush: for spreading warm klisters and for mixing klisters on skis.

Awl: for general repairs to pole straps and boots; an aid in mounting bindings.

Piece of terrycloth toweling: for drying ski bases.

Multiblade knife: all-around tool, useful for everything from ski repairs to opening bottles for post-race celebrations or wakes.

Pencil, small pocket notebook: to make notes on waxing, etc.

Paper towels: to clean up any mess left after waxing.

Some newspapers: to protect floor from waxing mess.

Nylon scouring pad: useful in cleaning skis.

Band-aids: for cut or burned fingers.

Soap and small hand towel: to wash hands after waxing, as even the best of waterless hand cleaners leave the hands slightly oily.

Second pocket waxing thermometer: because small waxing thermometers, like ball-point pens, are easily misplaced or lost.

Extra pole baskets and heat glue to put them on.

It is illegal and extremely dangerous to take on board an airplane or check with your luggage any hazardous materials.

CAUTION

Specific instructions for shipping these materials safely by air can be obtained from your airline cargo office.

Aerosols —polishes, degreasers, cleaners, etc. *(Exception:* maximum of 75 oz. toiletries, medicines in containers of up to 16 oz.)

Corrosives —acids, cleaners, wet batteries, etc.

Flammables —paints, thinners, lighter fluid, liquid reservoir lighters, cleaners, adhesives, etc.

Explosives—fireworks, flares, signal devices, loaded firearms, etc. *(Exception:* small arms ammunition for personal use securely packed in fiberboard, wood, or metal boxes inside checked baggage, NOT permitted in carry-on baggage.)

Radioactives —betascopes, radiopharmaceuticals, pacemakers not installed, etc.

Compressed Gases —tear gas or protective type sprays, oxygen cylinder, divers tanks, etc.

Loose Book Matches and/or Safety Matches *(Exception:* may be carried on person only.)

Poisons and Etiologic Agents (e.g., toxins).

Each violation can result in a civil penalty of up to $10,000 or a criminal penalty of not more than $25,000 and/or five years in jail for the individual and the employer.

U.S. Department of Transportation
Federal Aviation Administration

FAA caveat: gas is grounded!

About the Author

Other books by Michael Brady

Nordic Touring and Cross-Country Skiing
The Complete Ski Cross Country
Cross-Country Ski Gear
Citizen Racing (with John Caldwell)
Sequence Exercise (with Hans Gunnart and Olav Evjenth)

Translations

Physiology of Cross-Country Ski Racing, by Ulf Bergh
Teaching Children to Ski, by Flemmen and Grosvold

Editing

Edited SKINYTT, Norwegian Ski Instructors Association Journal
1968–70
Edited Guide to Cross-Country Skiing 1971–75

Other writing

Has written about 150 magazine articles on cross-country skiing, appearing in US, Canadian, Australian, Norwegian and Swedish skiing publications. Regular-column and short essays in SCANORAMA, SAS in-flight magazine

Coaching

Certified Norwegian Ski Instructor 1964
Certified Norwegian Cross-Country Ski Racing Coach 1965
Taught cross country ski-racing coaching workshops in US and Australia
Taught skiing in US, Australia, Canada and Norway